PLACES
OF
WORSHIP

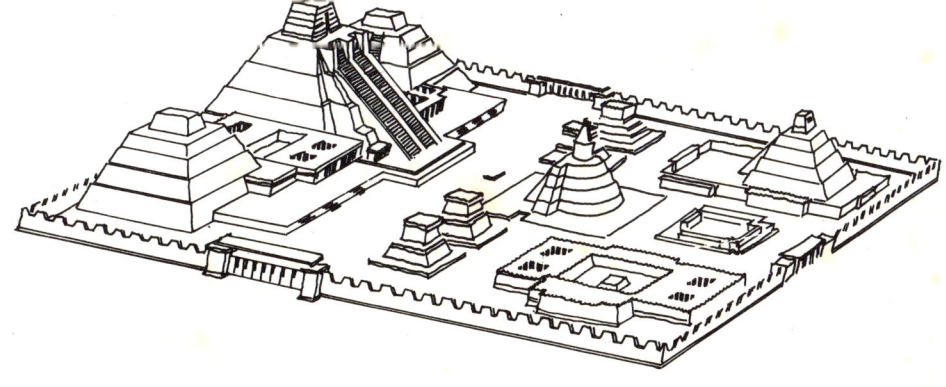

PLACES OF WORSHIP — Ancient Near East

For centuries the history of architecture has been monopolised by the places built for worship. Before 3000 B.C. the Egyptians rarely used stone, except for foundations. Timber, once quite plentiful, was used for the better buildings. Palm logs were used for roofs and the walls were of sun-dried mud brick. Cut stone was used only for the finest religious buildings. Even palaces remained comparatively frail.

Elsewhere in the Near East palace architecture was as important as temple architecture, but in Egypt monumental building was expressed largely in pyramids, tombs and temples. The Ancient Egyptians, great believers in afterlife, attempted to build lasting tombs to preserve the body and various goods necessary for the eternal enjoyment of the deceased. The three main types of tombs were mastabas, royal pyramids and rock hewn tombs.

Temples were of two main types: mortuary temples for the deceased pharaohs, and cult temples for the worship of ancient gods, such as the Temple of Khons, Karnack. Cult temples were characterised by entrance pylons, court, hypostyle hall, sanctuary and various chapels, all enclosed by a high wall. Temple decoration was usually pictures scratched on the mud-plaster walls. Columns were modelled on bundles of plant stems, and capitals were derived from the lotus bud, papyrus flower and the palm tree.

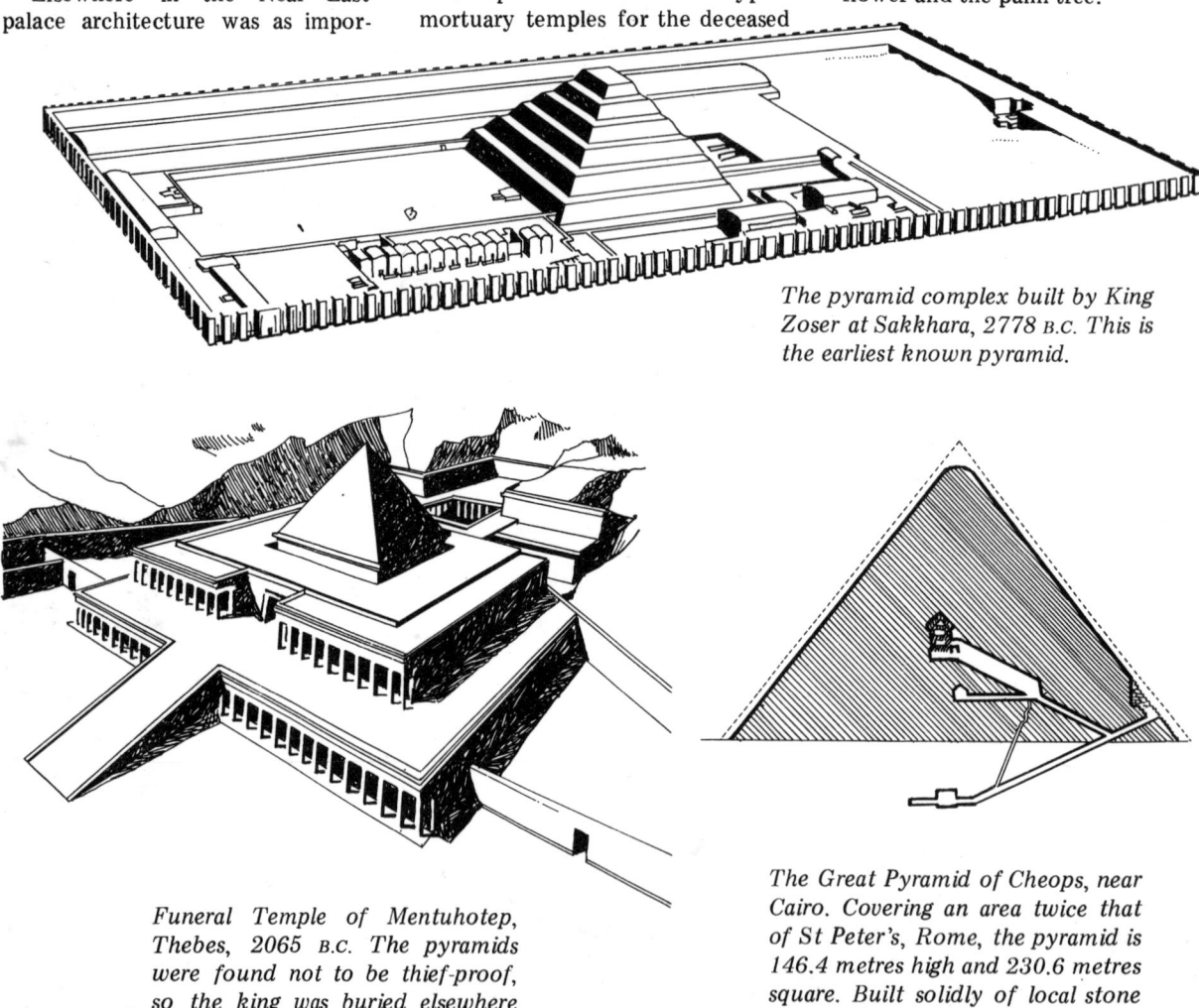

The pyramid complex built by King Zoser at Sakkhara, 2778 B.C. This is the earliest known pyramid.

Funeral Temple of Mentuhotep, Thebes, 2065 B.C. The pyramids were found not to be thief-proof, so the king was buried elsewhere and the pyramid became a symbolic tombstone.

The Great Pyramid of Cheops, near Cairo. Covering an area twice that of St Peter's, Rome, the pyramid is 146.4 metres high and 230.6 metres square. Built solidly of local stone with, originally, a covering of Turu limestone. Each block weighed 2500 kilogrammes. Additional buildings included an offering chapel and mortuary temple.

Mammisi Temple, Island of Elephantine, 1408 B.C.

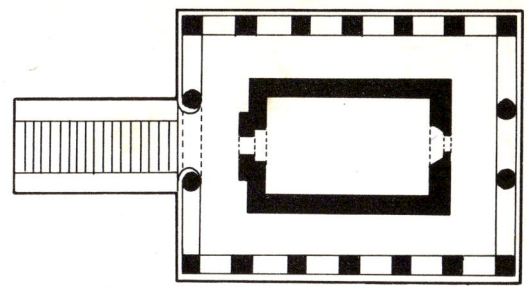
Typical small temple that usually stood in the outer enclosures of large temples

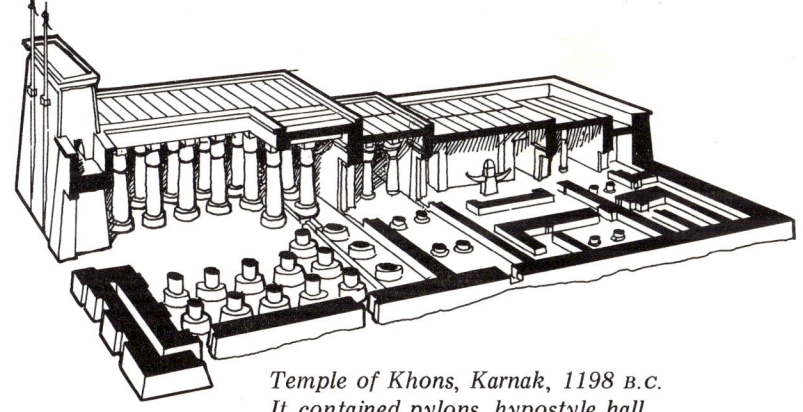

Temple of Khons, Karnak, 1198 B.C. It contained pylons, hypostyle hall and sanctuary.

Courtyard of the Temple of Khons

Hypostyle hall of the Great Temple of Ammon, Karnak, 1530-323 B.C.

Typical Egyptian columns, capitals, and bases

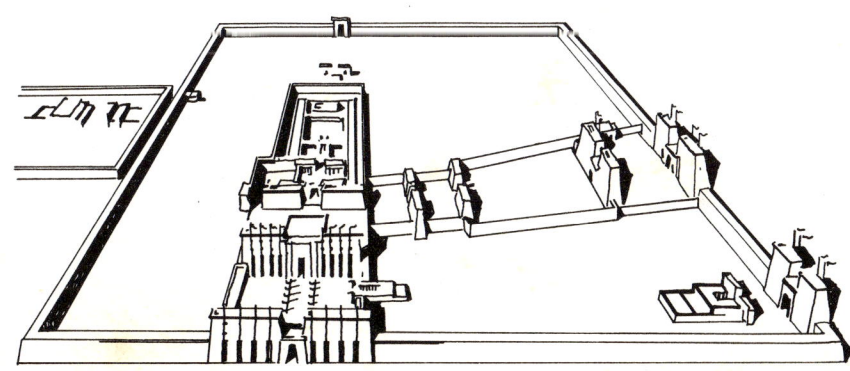
Great Temple of Ammon, Karnak. This was the grandest of all Egyptian temple complexes. There were six pairs of pylons, various courts, and halls leading to the sanctuary.

PLACES OF WORSHIP   Ancient Near East

The outstanding constructions along the river plains of the Tigris and Euphrates were the temple complexes and palaces. Stone and timber were rare, but there was plenty of river clay, which was moulded into bricks for every kind of structure. The buildings were raised on mud-brick platforms. The sacred ziggurats, made of tiered rectangular stages, belonged to the chief temples. The idea of making the religious ritual nobler by raising the shrine in which it took place continued through Sumerian times and reached its highest point in the ziggurat towers of Babylon and Assyria.

The main sanctuary was incorporated in a complex of subsidiary chambers and courtyards. At Khafaje, north-east of Baghdad, the main shrine stood on its own platform in the centre of an oval-shaped area protected by double walls and entered through a formal courtyard.

Walls were usually whitewashed or, as on some ziggurats, painted in colour. Colossal winged bulls guarded the main doors. Facing with multicoloured glazed bricks was introduced by the Assyrians in place of sculptured stone decoration because stone was scarce.

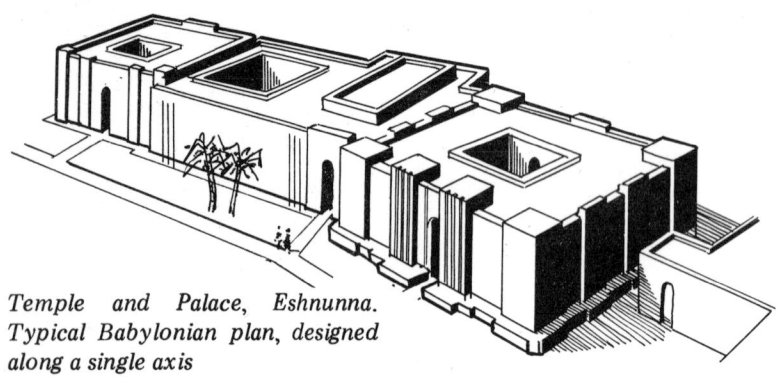

Temple and Palace, Eshnunna. Typical Babylonian plan, designed along a single axis

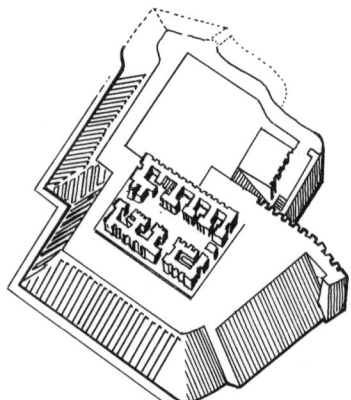

The White Temple, Uruk, 3500–3000 B.C. The temple stood on a 12 metre high platform. The later ziggurat, or temple-tower, originated here. The temple, originally whitewashed, dominated Uruk, the largest Sumerian city.

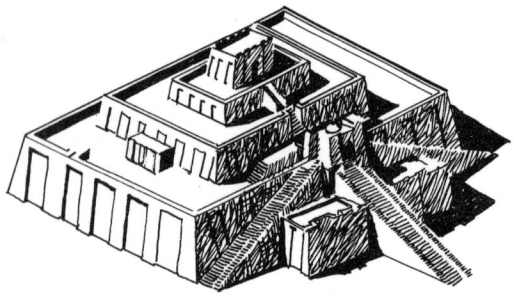

View of the Ziggurat of Urnammu, Ur, c. 2125 B.C.

Plan and view of the ziggurat at Tchoga-Zanbil, Elam, 13th century B.C.

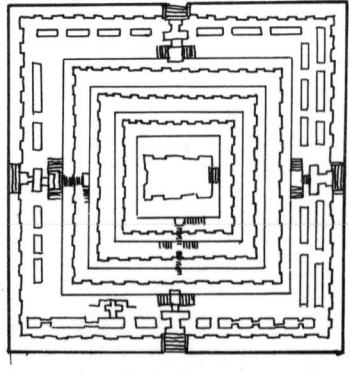

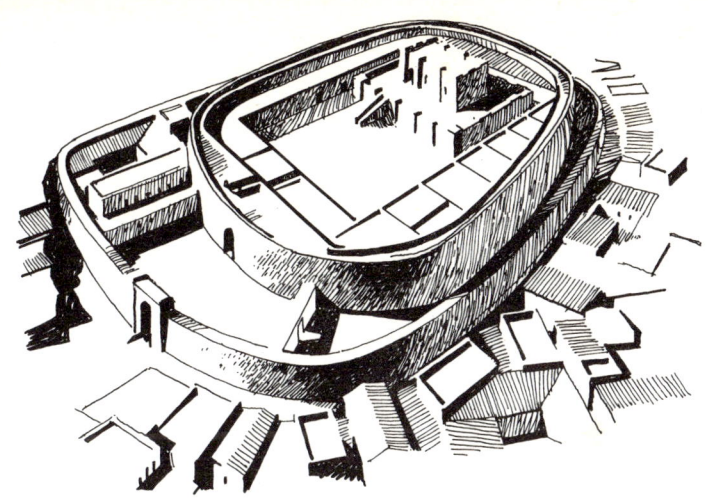

The temple oval at Khafaje, northeast of Baghdad, c. 3000 B.C.

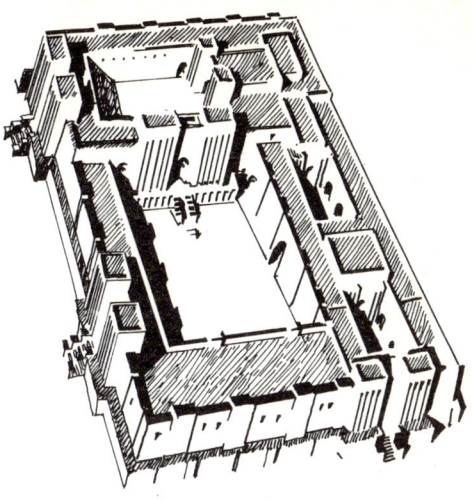

Temple complex, Ischali, c. 2000 B.C. It consisted of two terrace courts. The temple was built in the upper court at right angles to the main axis.

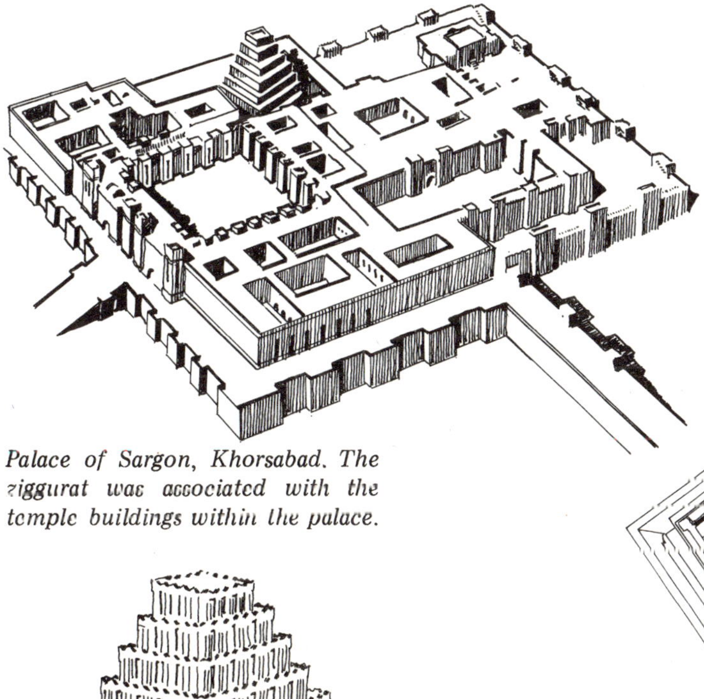

Churchill College, Cambridge, England. This project was designed in 1958 by James Stirling. It is a complex of college buildings planned within a great court. The historical traditions of such an idea go back to the palace temples of Assyria and the great temple complexes of Egypt; all that is missing are the great entrance pylons.

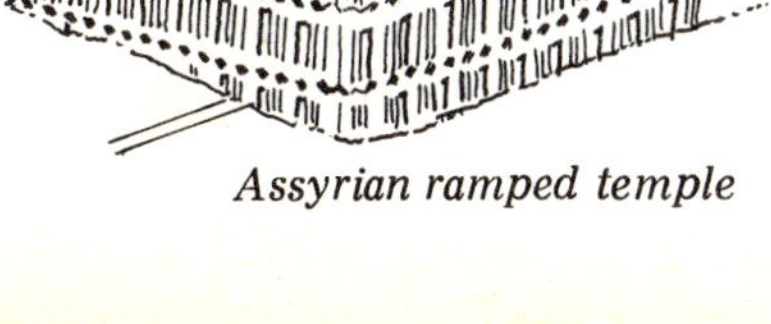

Palace of Sargon, Khorsabad. The ziggurat was associated with the temple buildings within the palace.

Assyrian ramped temple

PLACES OF WORSHIP Ancient Classical

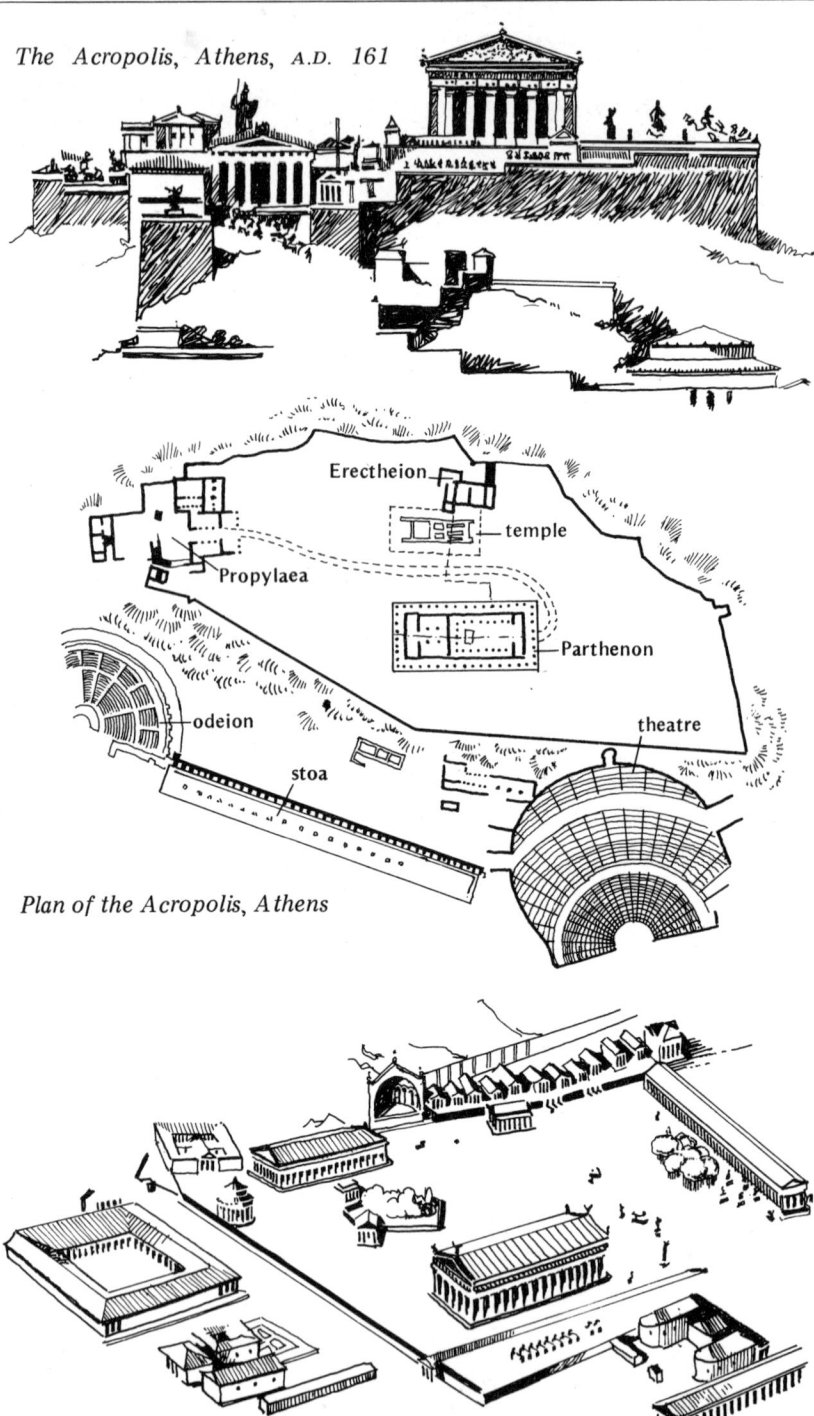

The Acropolis, Athens, A.D. 161

Plan of the Acropolis, Athens

View of Olympia, 2nd century A.D.

In the later Greek cities the major communal spaces were the sacred enclosures, as at Olympia. Some, like the Acropolis, or upper city, in Athens, were fortified citadels where the principal sacred buildings might stand. The sacred precincts usually contained a principal temple and one or two secondary temples and shrines. There were colonnaded shelters (the stoas), statues or votive columns in honour of heroes and philanthropists, walled recesses for rest and contemplation, and a sacred grove of trees.

The temple was the most important form in Greek architecture. It was built to house a particular god, not the worshippers. The earliest examples were rectangular halls with porches at the front supported on columns, and were based on the Minoan megaron (the main room of the house). The Greek desire for symmetry resulted in a second porch at the far end. The cult statue was enclosed in a central room. Later, a small room, to act as a treasury, was added. This became the basic form for later temples.

By the 5th century changes were not so much in form but in detail. The temples were, by tradition, rectangular, with a portico at each end and a surrounding colonnade. Windows were rare. The central entrance door was placed so that sunlight would light the cult statue.

Worshippers stayed near the altar, which was placed outside, and so temples were designed for external effect. The main characteristics were the orders of columns and capitals. Early Aegean and Greek temples used the Doric order, which had a timber origin. The Ionic order was used for the larger temples in Asia Minor, and the Corinthian order, which was a development of the decorative Egyptian columns and capitals, was common in later Hellenistic Greece.

Temple of Poseidon, Paestum, c. 460 B.C.

The Parthenon, Athens, 447–432 B.C. View and plan

East facade of the Parthenon, restored

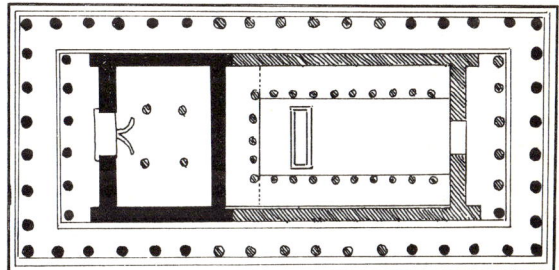

Temple of Artemis, Ephesus, c. 356 B.C. One of the most impressive Greek temples, celebrated for its sculpture

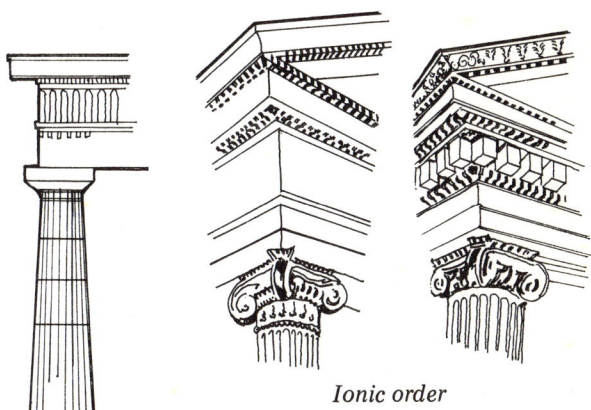

Doric order

Ionic order

The Erechtheion, Athens, 421–405 B.C.

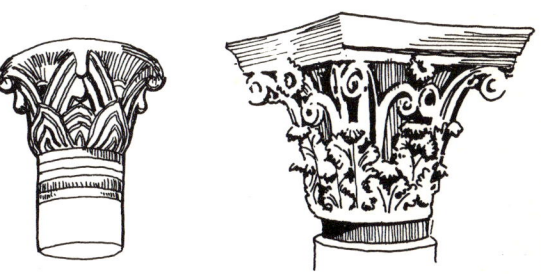

Evolution of the Corinthian capital from the Egyptian bell capital

PLACES OF WORSHIP Ancient Classical

Roman temples were a mixture of Greek and Etruscan temple design. The Etruscans occupied west-central Italy, known as Etruria, in ancient times. Originally immigrants from Asia Minor, they had established themselves as the greatest power in Italy by the 8th century B.C. Rome was little more than an insignificant hill town in southern Etruria in the 6th century B.C. By 500 B.C. Etruscan power in Rome had collapsed. As Etruscan fortunes declined, Roman influence and domination over Italy increased.

The Roman temples resembled the Greek in many respects, but the characteristic prostyle portico (a single row of columns at the front) and the use of a raised podium were Etruscan. The steps to the principal entrance were usually flanked by massive low walls adorned with statuary. The Maison Carrée, Nimes is a typical Roman temple. Instead of a peripteral (a single line of columns surrounding the central room), the side colonnades were replaced by half-columns attached to the walls with a prostyle portico in front. The central room of the Greeks, the cella, was widened, usually occupying the whole width of the temple.

Roman temples were generally isolated in precincts, as was the Temple of Mars Ultor in the Forum of Augustus. Entrances were emphasised by deep porticos and steps.

Etruscan temple, 3rd century B.C. A sloping ramp leads up to a portico with two columns. A central door opens into the main room.

Temple of Mars Ultor in the Forum of Augustus, 14-2 B.C.

Maison Carrée, Nimes, 16 B.C. The best preserved Roman temple in existence

Temple of Venus and Rome, Rome, A.D. 123-35. Like the temple complexes of the ancient Near East, it was raised on a platform.

Temple of Vesta, Rome, A.D. 205

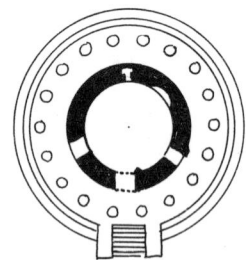
Temple of Vesta, Tivoli, c. 80 B.C.

The Temple of Vesta in Rome stood in the Forum Romanum and was the most sacred shrine of the city. It was here the Vestal Virgins kept alight the sacred fire, which signified the home hearth as the centre and source of Roman life and power.

Temple at Baalbeck, Lebanon, 2nd century A.D. The interior is remarkably ornate, in contrast to the Greek tradition for plainness.

The circular Temple of Portunus (c. 31 B.C.) and the Temple of Fortuna Virilis (c. 40 B.C.) in the Forum Boarium, Rome

Section of the Pantheon, Rome

Entrance to Pantheon

Interior of Pantheon

Corinthian Order

The Pantheon is the most famous circular temple. It was rebuilt as a rotunda by the Emperor Hadrian (A.D. 120–124) on the site of an older temple. It was erected on the forecourt to the older temple at a higher level so that the podium of the latter could serve as foundations for a boldly projecting porch. Hadrian reused the portico of the older temple, but made it octostyle (8 columns) instead of decastyle (10 columns) as in the original. The ancient bronze doors, which still remain, were plated with gold. The dome is the largest ever built, having a diameter of 43.43 metres. Inside, the walls were lined with marble and porphyry. The building was lit by one circular unglazed opening, 8 metres in diameter, in the crown of the magnificent coffered dome. In A.D. 608 the temple was rededicated as a Christian church.

PLACES OF WORSHIP   Ancient Far East

The Indian temple is planned around its cella, a small unlit shrine. It is crowned with a spire-shaped roof formed of horizontal courses of stone. It is approached by one or more porch-like halls used for religious dancing and music. The vertical spire, the sikhara, like the church tower in the English countryside, proclaims the holy place. In northern India the sikhara is very dominant, and the porch hall is usually enclosed by screens. In central India the temples are more elaborate in form and decoration. In the south the spire becomes a flatter pyramid with straight or concave sides.

Indian culture, based on Hinduism and Buddhism, spread throughout south-east Asia as a result of colonialism. The adoption of Indian culture abroad is seen best in the temple-mountain of Borobudur, Java and the temple complex of Angkor Wat, Cambodia.

Stupas and monumental pillars, free-standing like the Pillars of Victory in the Acropolis and Roman Forum, are characteristic of Buddhist architecture. The Hindus and Buddhists did not learn to enclose large spaces until late and so, with the exception of audience halls and passageways, the architecture is designed, like the Greek temple, for purely external effect. Buddhist temples in China resemble those of India. They consist of open courts and porticoes with refectories and accommodation for the priests. The most important structures in the temple enclosures are the pagodas. Originally religious in importance, they sometimes later became monuments to victory.

Japanese temples, influenced by Chinese, are more symmetrical in composition with elaborately decorated interiors. The temples are usually isolated structures within a concentric enclosure.

The Temple of Brahmeswara, Orissa, India, 9th century

Temple of the Sun, Konarak, Orissa, 13th century

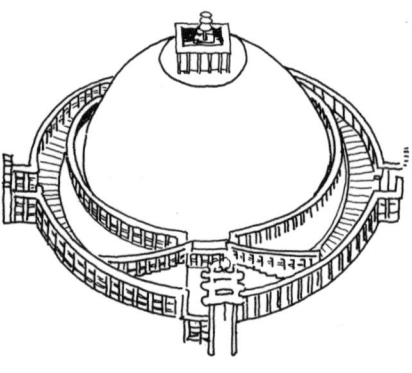

The Great Stupa, Sanchi, India, 2nd century

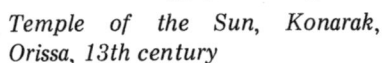

The Buddhist temple-mountain built at Borobudur, Java, c. A.D. 800

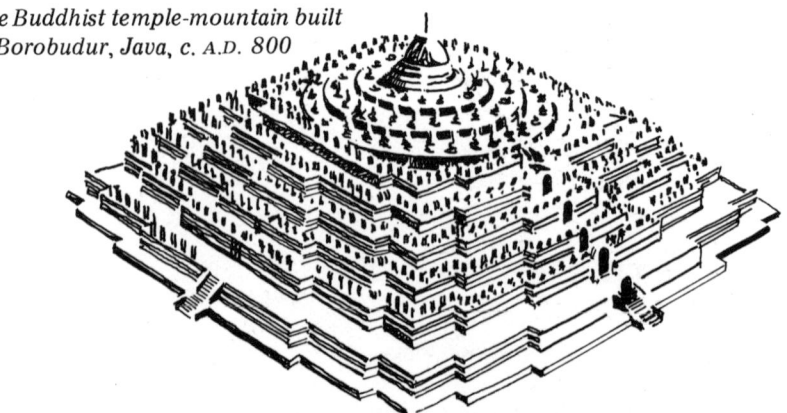

The Swayambhunath Stupa, Katmandu, Nepal. The 13 diminishing tiers on the spire symbolise the 13 Buddhist heavens.

The Temple of Angkor Wat, Cambodia, 12th century

Wat Pichayat, Bangkok, Thailand

Lung-hsing Temple, Cheng-ting-hsien, Hopei, China, 11th century

Ch'i-nien Tien, Peking, 1540

Pagoda, Fo-kung Ssu, Shansi, China, 1056

Hiryu-ji Temple, Nara, Japan, A.D. c. 607

PLACES OF WORSHIP — Byzantine and Medieval

The early Christians met in the converted rooms of private houses or tenements. The first Christian churches were the basilican churches, such as St Peter's and Santa Maria Maggiore, Rome. These were usually built over the burial-place of the saint to whom the church was dedicated. Their model was the basilica, the Roman exchange and halls of justice, such as the Basilica of Trajan, Rome. And so the basilican church becomes a link between pagan classical times and the Romanesque period that was to follow. Curiously, this link extends further still, to the bible lands of the ancient Near East. Here the business side of the Roman basilica was conducted in the temple itself. It was this same temple of God into which Jesus went to cast out the buyers, sellers, and moneychangers. He wanted his house to be a house of prayer and not a den of thieves. With such association, it is amazing that the basilican churches of Christian Rome flourished. But then where else were the larger congregations to meet? No other building type had developed such an accommodating structure, whether for pagan or Christian needs. The approach to these churches was usually through an atrium, an open court surrounded by arcades.

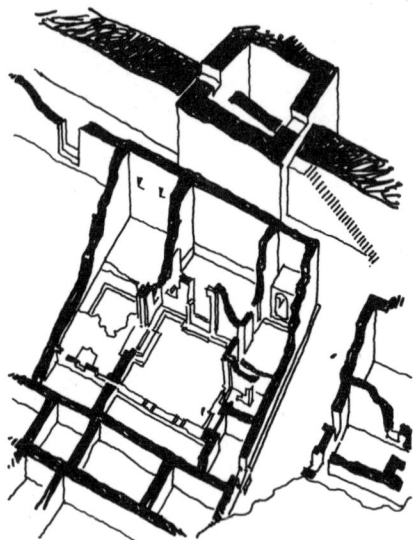

Christians in 3rd and 4th century Rome met in converted private residences. The use of domestic houses was partly an attempt to do without the official and religious architecture of the time, with all its pagan association, and partly to avoid harassment by the authorities, which the early Christians suffered. The house illustrated is at Dura-Europas. It was converted to a Christian community house in A.D. 231. Two rooms on the south were converted to one room and seated a congregation of 50 or 60.

Basilica of Trajan, Rome, A.D. 98-112

Basilican church of Santa Maria Maggiore, Rome, A.D. 432

Basilican church of St Peter, Rome, A.D. 330

Exterior and interior of San Agnese Fuori Le Mura, Rome, A.D. 625-38

San Apollinare in Classe, Ravenna, A.D. 534-9

St Catherine's Monastery, Mount Sinai, mid-6th century. Built as a fortress shrine, the complex consists of a church, additional buildings and barracks for the protecting garrison, and is enclosed by a high wall.

San Stefano Rotondo, Rome, A.D. 468-83

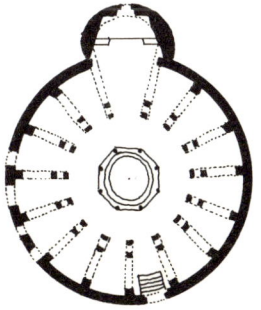

Baptistry, Nocera, mid-4th-6th century

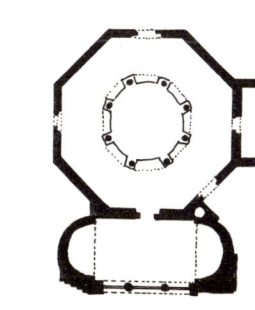

Baptistry of Constantine, Rome, A.D. 442-40

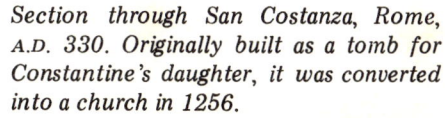

Section through San Costanza, Rome, A.D. 330. Originally built as a tomb for Constantine's daughter, it was converted into a church in 1256.

| PLACES OF WORSHIP | **Byzantine and Medieval** |

Byzantium, later renamed Constantinople and finally Istanbul, was founded as a Greek colony about 660 B.C. and became the capital of the Roman Empire in A.D. 330. When the Empire was finally divided in 395, Byzantium continued to be the capital of the Eastern Empire. Throughout the Middle Ages it was the bulwark of Christianity against attacks from the Muslims on the east and the Slavs on the west.

Whereas the early Christians developed the timber roof trusses and basilican plan, the Byzantines developed a dome shaped roof to cover square and many-sided churches, baptistries and tombs. The system of hand-laid concrete construction introduced by the Romans became more like brickwork, and in this form was later adopted by the Byzantines. Externally, the brickwork was increasingly used for decorative patterns and bandings. Ornamental stone bands and decorative arches were introduced. The churches usually had a dome over the nave. Byzantine churches in Greece were much smaller, the dome was raised on a drum, and there were additional smaller domes at a lower level. The buildings of this period in Ravenna, Italy are particularly Byzantine in character. The influence of Byzantium was carried west along the trade routes by Venetian merchants and so it is not surprising to see similarities between St Font, Perigueux and St Mark's, Venice.

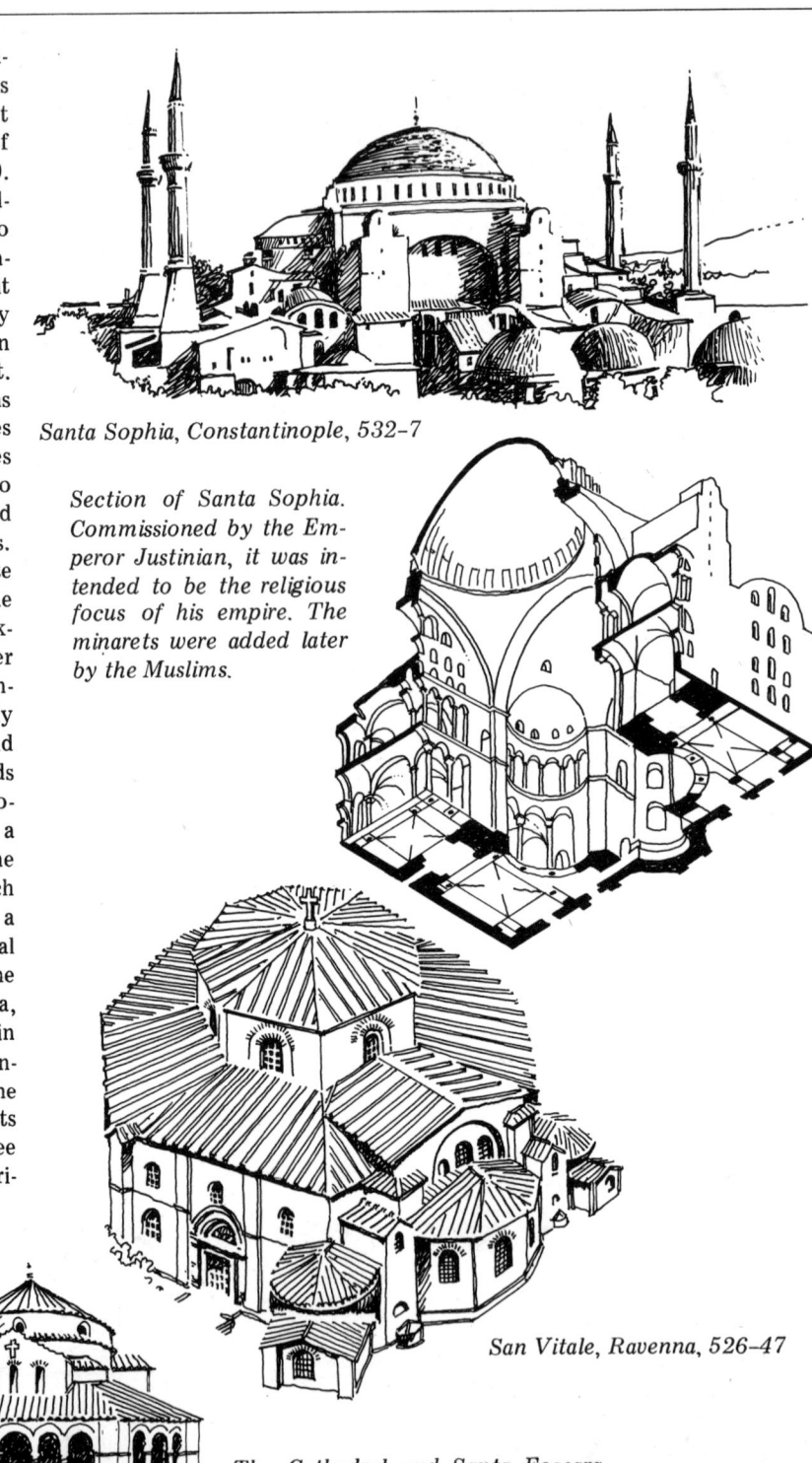

Santa Sophia, Constantinople, 532-7

Section of Santa Sophia. Commissioned by the Emperor Justinian, it was intended to be the religious focus of his empire. The minarets were added later by the Muslims.

San Vitale, Ravenna, 526-47

The Cathedral and Santa Foscara Church, Torcello, 1108, built on an island in the lagoons of Venice

St Mark's, Venice, 1063–85. Situated midway between east and west, the merchant city of Venice reflected the art of Byzantium in this great cathedral.

Section through St Mark's

Section through St Font, Perigueux. An almost identical copy in plan of St Mark's

Church of Gorgeopekos, Athens, 9th–13th century

Church of Kapnikarea, Athens, 9th–13th century

Church of St Nicholas, Rumania, c. 1330

Cathedral of St Basil, Red Square, Moscow, 1554-1679

Cathedral of the Assumption, Vladimir, USSR, 12th century

Cathedral of the Assumption, the Kremlin, 1475–79

PLACES OF WORSHIP — The Islamic World

Unlike other buildings for worship, the mosque of the Islamic world was neither a dwelling house of the deity (god), as in the Roman or Greek temples, nor a sanctuary in the Christian sense. The mosque was simply the meeting place of the faithful.

Within 80 years of Muhammad's death in 632, a number of great congregational mosques had been built. Many mosques were used both as schools and places of business. Public notices were announced there, and travellers from the newly-arrived caravans normally went to the mosque, where they had a right of shelter.

Most Islamic buildings were built around a principal axis, which often extended into the formal landscape that is a basic part of the designs. The courtyard, a major feature of the congregational mosque, is also used in the madrassah (college), the hostel (caravanserai), the palace, and the house. Architectural features include both timber and masonry arcading, the distinctive pointed arch, the dome, and columns. The decorative finishes include ceramic cladding, interlocking timber panels of geometric patterns, and the use of calligraphy.

The Islamic influence in India was a result of the Islamic conquest in the late 13th century. The most famous example of Indo-Islamic architecture is the Taj Mahal, a mausoleum built by the Emperor Shah Jehan for his favourite wife.

Dome of the Rock, Jerusalem 688–92. One of the most important Islamic structures, it consists of a great central dome covering the summit of Mount Moriah, whence the Prophet is believed to have made his night ride to Heaven.

Ibn Tulun Mosque, Cairo, 876–9, is the finest surviving congregational mosque.

The Masjid-i-Shah, the Imperial Mosque, Isfahan, begun in 1612

Mosque of Sultan Ahmed, Istanbul, 1610–16

Taj Mahal, Agra, 1630–53

PLACES OF WORSHIP   **The Ancient Americas**

Much of the temple architecture of the ancient Americas was based on the gigantic pyramid temple, the Pyramid of the Moon, built in the city of Teotihuacan about the time of Christ. The three great races here were the Aztecs, the Mayas and the Incas. Little remains of Aztec architecture, not so much because they were warriors rather than builders, but because their city, Tenochtitlan, was destroyed by the Spanish conquistadors under Cortes in 1521. Both the Aztecs and the Mayas practised human sacrifice, and height and mass were of vital importance in ceremonial buildings designed to strike awe and terror in people. The Mayas were the more gifted people architecturally, although their ignorance of the arch meant they couldn't build high with ease. The only way the architects could solve this problem was by building huge mounds with pyramids on top crowned with tiny temples. The Maya talent was for decoration, proportion and design. The Incas of the Peruvian Andes were less artistic, but they were the best stone masons the world has ever known.

Temple built at Palenque, a hilltop city built by the Mayas

Columns from temples built by the Toltecs in central Mexico, 10th century

El Castillo. This temple pyramid was built in the late 12th century in the Toltec-Maya city of Chichon Itza, in Yucatan

Pyramid of the Moon, begun in the 1st century A.D. in the city of Teotihuacan

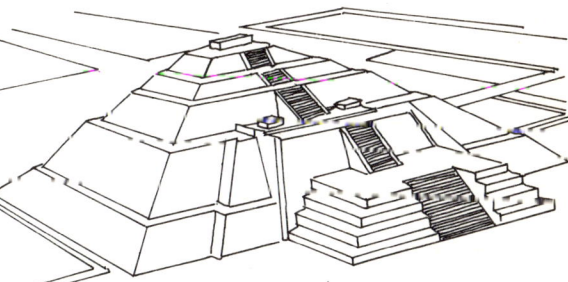

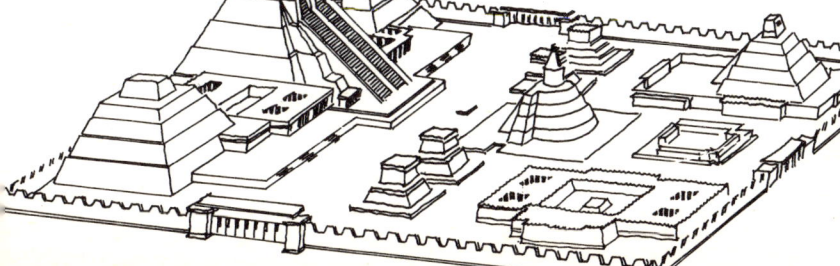

Tenochtitlan, the city of Montezuma and the ancient capital of the Aztecs, was built on an island in Lake Texcoco. It was begun in 1325.

PLACES OF WORSHIP — Byzantine and Medieval

During the Romanesque period in central Italy the basilican type of church still predominated. While the Italians allowed the architectural form to be governed by the classical tradition of the Roman basilica, they became much more preoccupied with the beauty and delicacy of ornamental detail.

The ornamental arcades that adorned the facades were a characteristic feature. These arcaded galleries, as used at Pisa, were purely decorative. Walls faced in marble were a feature that distinguished Italian Romanesque architecture from that of the rest of Europe. The small doors and windows, designed to shut out the bright light, are unimportant. Timber roofs continued the tradition of the basilican type, while hundreds of columns from ancient Roman temples were reused. In France, and other places more remote from Rome, novel types of columns were developed.

The principal innovation in northern Italy was the development of the ribbed vault. The churches were still of the basilican type, but the nave and aisles were vaulted. Aisles were often two storeys high. Externally, the division between nave and aisle was masked by a flat entrance facade built in front of the whole church. Towers (campaniles), often detached, were common.

The Baptistry, Parma, 1196-1296

Trani Cathedral, Apulia, Italy, c. 1094

Pisa Cathedral, 1063-1118, and the Baptistry, 1153-1265

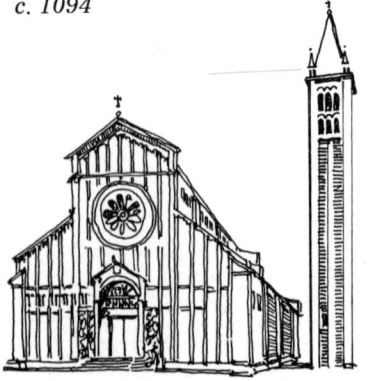

Church of San Zeno, Verona, Italy, begun 1140

San Michele, Lucca, Italy, begun 1140

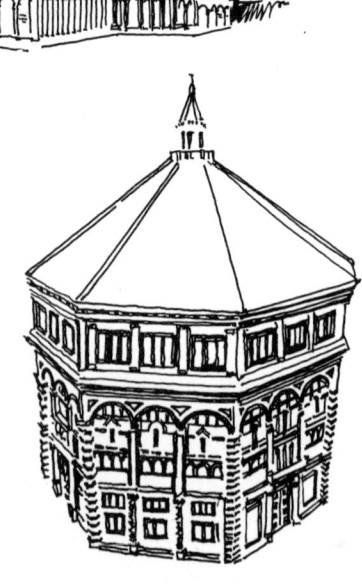

The Baptistry, Florence, 5th-13th century

Circular churches were rare in France, but the development of a semicircular east end as an ambulatory (an aisle or sanctuary) was common in southern France. Churches were usually cruciform in plan and frequently had naves covered with barrel vaults. Towers were sometimes detached, as in Italy. Facades were richly decorated, and many churches had elaborate cloisters. Many piers and capitals were derived from Roman models. Roofs were usually low in pitch, but eastern Mediterranean influences resulted in the domical forms at Angouleme. In the north the nave and aisle of the basilican church predominated. Churches in Normandy were characterised by the introduction of two flanking towers. Windows with semicircular heads were often grouped together and enclosed under one arch. Massive walls were a characteristic of the French Romanesque style. Facades were often broken by a distinctive line of bricks (string course) or horizontal mouldings. The stone mouldings were coarser than the marble mouldings of Italy. Decorative carvings were usually of foliage or figures of animals or men.

St Sernin, Toulouse, France, 1077-1119

Notre Dame la Grande, Poitiers, France, 1130-45

Angouleme Cathedral, France, 1105-28

Abbaye-aux-Hommes (known as St Etiennes), Caen, 1058-1115; a product of the prosperity and power of the Norman dukes

Abbaye-aux-Dames, Caen, 1062-1110

PLACES OF WORSHIP — Byzantine and Medieval

Anglo-Saxon and Romanesque architecture in Britain was inevitably influenced by Roman architecture. Christian churches built in Britain before the end of the Roman occupation were of the basilican type. Following the departure of the Romans in A.D. 410, much of their architecture was destroyed by the invading barbarians. By the late 8th century Saxon kings and their people had been converted to Christianity and numerous churches had been built. Many buildings were composed of either fragments or rough copies of Roman architectural details. Arches were semicircular, and windows had either round or triangular heads. Vaulting was plain and simple. A characteristic feature were wall angles in long and short work, and pilaster strips.

The English Romanesque, or Norman, architecture (1066-1189) was bold and massive, with semicircular arches, heavy cylindrical piers and flat buttresses. Windows were small and deeply splayed, and elaborately carved mouldings surrounded the openings of doors and windows. Rib vaulting, which replaced groin vaulting, was introduced. The nave was lengthened, and towers were square and massive.

Earls Barton church tower

Sompting church tower, Sussex

Details of Anglo-Saxon church windows

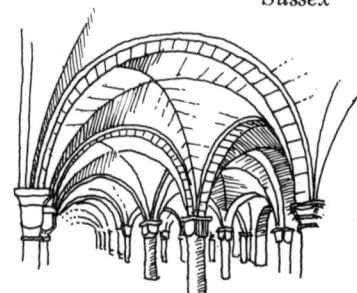

Norman vaulting: groined vault, Canterbury crypt

Ribbed wall, Peterborough Cathedral

Durham Cathedral, begun 1096. The Norman nave is the finest in England.

Southwell Minster, c. 1130

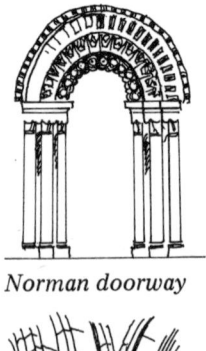

Norman doorway

Typical Norman capital

The Roman cross-vaults were used throughout Europe until the beginning of the 12th century, but they were heavy and difficult to construct and eventually were replaced by the rib and panel vaulting.

Romanesque churches in Germany were peculiar in having both eastern and western apses, and so there are no great entrances in the west, as in French churches. Characteristic features were the numerous circular and octagonal turrets, many-sided domes, and arcaded galleries under the eaves.

Little Romanesque architecture survives in Belgium, but Tournai Cathedral is one of the finest Romanesque buildings in Europe.

St Mary's, Maastricht, is the major Romanesque church in Holland. Most Romanesque buildings in eastern Europe were built of less substantial materials and, therefore, little survives.

Church of the Apostles, Cologne, c. 1190

Speyer Cathedral, 1031-61

Worms Cathedral, 11th-12th century

Tournai Cathedral, Belgium, 1066-1338

Trier Cathedral, 1016-47

St Mary's, Maastricht, Holland, begun 10th century

Romanesque doorway of the Old Cathedral, Coimbra, Portugal

PLACES OF WORSHIP   Byzantine and Medieval

Gothic architecture was the predominant form of building in Western Europe from about 1200 until the beginning of the Renaissance, or rebirth of Roman architecture, which started in Italy in the 15th century and in the rest of Europe in the 16th century. The circular arches, heavy columns and massive walls of the Romanesque gave way to the pointed arch, rib vault, flying buttress, and the use of spacious arcades, galleries and clerestory windows to reduce the area of wall of Gothic architecture. In Italy the Roman tradition was so strong that there is little evidence of the vertical form and detail characteristic of northern Gothic. The German influence seen in Milan Cathedral was a direct result of the fact that a number of consultants employed in its design and construction came from north of the Alps. The vast quantity of decorative sculpture was carried out by Italian, French and German sculptors, but the bulk of the structural and engineering work was carried out by Germans. The Italians retained the basilican plan for their cathedrals and churches.

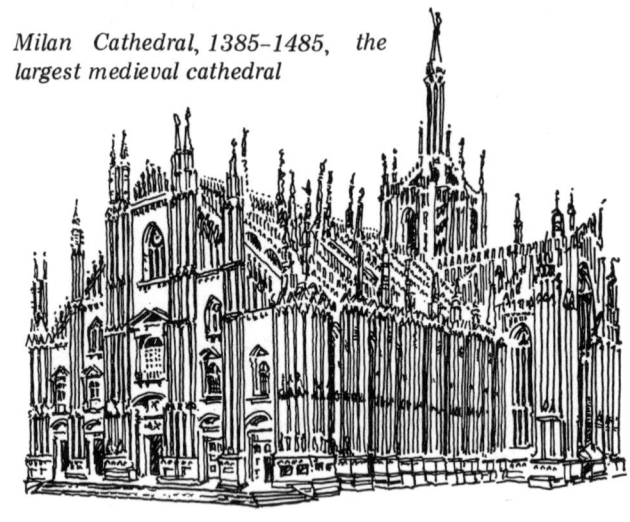

Milan Cathedral, 1385–1485, the largest medieval cathedral

Orvieto Cathedral, 1290–1600

Siena Cathedral, 1245–1380

The great pilgrimage church of San Francesco, Assisi, 1228–53

The difference between Gothic and Romanesque architecture was in the use of a vaulting framework of intersecting stone pointed-arch ribs supporting thin stone panels. The pressure of loads carried by the vaults was collected where the ribs met at the angles of the vaulting compartments. The pressure was then carried to the ground by buttresses and flying buttresses weighted by pinnacles. The use of the Gothic system of buttresses also meant that walls were no longer used to carry the loads imposed by the roof, and were now treated as decorative screen walls with the introduction of elaborate traceried windows. Few people could read and so, with the development of stained glass, the windows acted as a framework for illustrated Bible stories.

In England cathedrals were set apart in secluded closes and were usually part of a monastic establishment. In France cathedrals were part of the life of the town, serving not only for religious gatherings but as public meeting places. Most French cathedrals were intended to have many towers and spires, but few were built due to the engineering difficulties of adding such features to the vast, high buildings. English cathedrals were generally lower and smaller and could easily carry a tall spire.

Notre Dame, Paris, 1180–1330 It is one of the oldest of the French Gothic cathedrals.

Amiens Cathedral, 1220–88

Bayeux Cathedral, 13th–15th century

Mont St Michel, 13th century and later. A fortified monastery

St Ouen, Rouen, 1318–1515

Chartres Cathedral, 1194–1260

PLACES OF WORSHIP — Byzantine and Medieval

The problem for the medieval architect was to construct a stone vault over the lofty nave of a basilican church while leaving clerestory windows in the nave walls above the aisle roof. The Roman waggon vault, a semicircular intersecting vault, had been developed in the Romanesque period. Two intersecting vaults were developed from this.

The ribbed vault was developed in the Gothic period. By concentrating the weight of vaulted roofs onto stone ribs and counteracting the outward thrust of the ribs by means of bold buttresses it became possible to reduce the thickness of walls between buttresses and to pierce the walls with large windows.

English Gothic architecture is divided into three stages of development: Early English (1189-1307), Decorated (1307-77), and Perpendicular (1377-1485). Early English features were the pointed arch, tall, narrow lancet windows giving height to the buildings, projecting buttresses and groups of slender shafts replacing the massive Norman pillars.

In the Decorated period windows increased in size, and battlemented parapets and angle buttresses, set diagonally, were introduced. Window tracery consisted of geometric forms and curvilinear, or flowing, lines.

In the Perpendicular period window tracery and panelling were given vertical lines. Windows were further enlarged, and fan vaults, with their numerous ribs and panels, were introduced.

Evolution of Gothic vaulting

Roman waggon vaults

Romanesque vaults

Gothic sexpartite vault and ribbed vault

Lincoln Cathedral, 11th–14th century

Salisbury Cathedral, 1220–65

St John's, Glastonbury, c. 1485

Canterbury Cathedral, begun 1069

York Minster, 14th–15th century

Belgium Gothic architecture in the eastern, hilly part was influenced by Germany while the low-lying areas were influenced by France.

In Holland the churches were simple and barn-like in character. There was a national tendency for plainness, emphasised by the use of brick.

In northern Germany too the architecture was carried out in brick. There was a national preference for the heavy forms of German Romanesque, which explains the comparatively late development of German Gothic in the mid-13th century when the Gothic architecture of France was already at its peak. A special characteristic of northern Germany was the hall church where nave and aisles were of the same height.

In Spain the Moorish influence, seen in the horseshoe arch and pierced stone tracery, was strong until the expulsion of the Moors with the fall of Granada in 1492.

St Gudule, Brussels, 1220-1475

Cologne Cathedral, begun 1284

Ulm Cathedral, 1377-1492

Prague Cathedral, 1344-85

Cathedral of St Jan's, Hertogenbosch, Holland, 1419-1529

Skara Cathedral, Sweden, c. 1300

Burgos Cathedral, Spain, 1221-1475

Seville Cathedral, Spain, 1402-1520

PLACES OF WORSHIP   Classical

The Renaissance began in the world of literature with the writings of Petrarch, Dante and Boccaccio. It then developed with the expansion of universities, and found expression in sculpture and painting.

The first architect of the Renaissance was Brunelleschi, whose miracle of design was the blending of a Renaissance dome with the Gothic architecture of the cathedral in Florence. Alberti was the first architect of the Renaissance to use flanking scrolls in his design for the facade of the Gothic church of Santa Maria Novella.

These early 15th century works were followed by the purer, high Renaissance designs of Bramante. His Tempietto, Rome, a development of the circular Roman temple, is a classic of the high Renaissance style that demonstrates the Renaissance ability to mix pagan and Christian symbols. This purer style, developed under Bramante, was derived from the writings of the Roman architect Vitruvius.

Michelangelo's work was mainly Mannerist, a transitional style between high Renaissance and full Baroque. His greatest work was in the Basilica of St Peter, Rome. The major Italian architect of the late 16th century was Palladio. His work linked the classicism of Bramante and the mannerism of Michelangelo. His outstanding churches in Venice are Il Redentore and San Georgio Maggiore.

Santa Maria Novella, Florence, facade by Alberti, 1470

Dome of Florence Cathedral, by Brunelleschi, 1420-34

The Tempietto, Rome, by Bramante, 1502-10

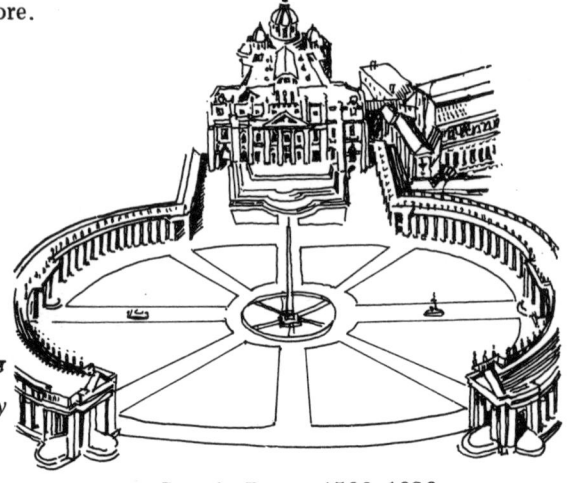
St Peter's, Rome, 1506-1626

Santa Maria della Salute, Venice, by Longhena, 1631-82

Il Redentore, Venice, by Palladio, 1577-92

San Georgio Maggiore, Venice, by Palladio, 1565

The Renaissance style in France began 80 years later than in Italy, but by the 17th century France had produced some of the finest buildings in Europe. The preference was for a more classical and less flamboyantly Baroque style of architecture. Decoration was delicate. The Church of the Sorbonne had two fine facades, both Roman in design. The most Baroque church in France was J. H. Mansart's design for Les Invalides. French Baroque was more classical than Italian. The dome is one of the most impressive Renaissance works in France. It has a diameter of 27.6 metres and is placed over the centre of a Greek-cross plan. The Madelaine, Paris, by Vignon, re-uses the Roman temple model complete with nave as the Roman cella. It was a forerunner to the eclecticism of the 19th century, when buildings were designed in a variety of styles reminiscent of all the great periods of architectural history.

Church of Val de Grace, begun by Mansart, 1645-65

Church of the Sorbonne, by Lemercier, 1635

The Madelaine, Paris, by Vignon, 1806-42

The Pantheon, Paris, by Soufflot, 1755-92

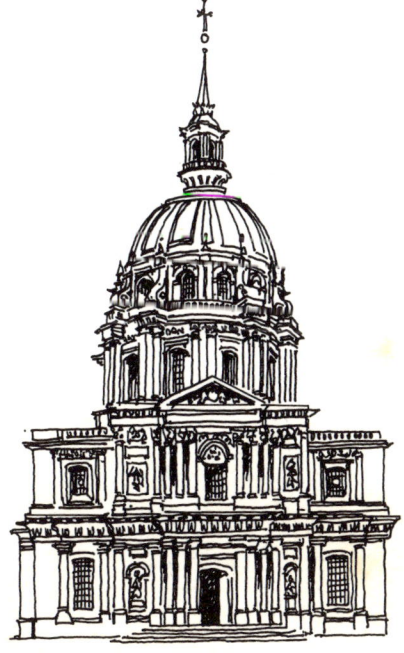

Les Invalides, Paris, by J. H. Mansart, 1680-91

Section through the dome of Les Invalides

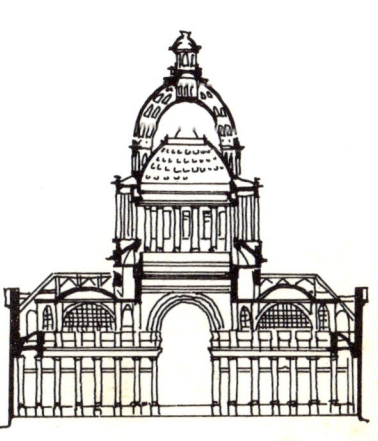

Section through the dome of the Pantheon

PLACES OF WORSHIP Classical

The Tudor period (1558-1603) was the first stage of the transition of English architecture from Gothic to Renaissance. There was little church building between the mid-16th and mid-17th centuries. This was the result of religious turmoil as well as the existence of a surplus of medieval churches, which was due partly to over-building during the Age of Faith, and partly to the dissolution of the monasteries by Henry VIII. The most influential church architect was Sir Christopher Wren, who was strongly influenced by the French Renaissance. Under Wren, classic features such as domes and columns were used to great effect. The destruction of much of the City of London in the Great Fire of 1666 gave Wren his great opportunity. The rebuilding of St Paul's was his masterpiece. Unlike St Peter's, Rome, which had 13 successive architects and numerous master masons and took over 100 years to build, St Paul's had one architect and one master mason and was completed in 35 years.

Wren rebuilt 52 of the city's churches. They were the first churches designed to meet the requirements of Protestant worship, having a central preaching space that usurped the nave and aisles. Galleries were a characteristic feature of these churches. The Wren classical tradition was developed by Gibbs, the outstanding architect of the early 18th century.

Section and facade St Paul's Cathedral, London, 1675-1710

St Paul's

Designed by Christopher Wren, it occupies the site of the medieval cathedral destroyed in the Great Fire of London. The central two-storeyed entrance portico is flanked by two magnificent towers, or campaniles, and the dome is probably the finest in Europe. Like all the great Renaissance architects, Wren quoted freely from the works of Serlio and Vitruvius.

St Vedast, by Wren, 1698

St Mary-le-Strand, by Gibbs, 1714-17

St Martin-in-the-Fields, by James Gibbs, 1722

In Spain the genuine classical style was established by Juan de Herrera (c. 1530-97), the architect of the Escorial, the great monastic palace on the hills near Madrid. The severity, simplicity and monumentality of his works were in complete contrast to the overdecorated buildings of early 16th century Spain. By the late 16th century the Italian Mannerist and Baroque traditions were beginning to have an effect, and by the 18th century the quantity of Baroque work in the cathedrals of Spain, such as Murcia Cathedral, was considerable. It was mostly the addition of new facades to medieval or Renaissance buildings. By now the Baroque was the major artistic form in much of central and eastern Europe.

In Germany the chief centres of the Baroque were Bamburg, Nuremberg and Wurzberg. The leading genius of this period of German Baroque was Balthasar Neumann (1687-1753). His major works are the pilgrimage church of Viezehnheiligen and the abbey church at Neresheim. The pilgrimage church is a classic masterpiece of German Baroque, with its tall striking exterior and superb interior. From 1740 onwards German Baroque began to be superseded by French Rococo and, later, the Neo-classical styles. The great architects of the Rococo period were Johann Zimmerman, J. M. Fischer, and the Acam brothers.

St Michael, Germany, 1607-27

Facade of Murcia Cathedral, Spain, by Jaime Bort y Meha, 1740-54

Karlskirche, Vienna, by Von Erlach, 1716

Pilgrimage Church of Vierzehnheiligen, by Balthazar Neumann, begun 1743

Carmelite Church, Hungary, 1725

The Escorial, Madrid, 1559-84. It consists of a college, monastery, church and palace.

The Frauenkirche, Dresden, 1726-40 (destroyed)

PLACES OF WORSHIP   The Modern World

The dilemma of the modern world was which way to turn, and the varied style in church building is a reasonable indication of this dilemma. Architects were at a crossroads. The Church of the Sacre Coeur clearly made reference to the Romanesque and Byzantine, and one would be forgiven for mistaking the Natural History Museum in London for yet another great cathedral. The church in Copenhagen is obviously religious—the church organ is expressed on the facade. Was this really what was wanted?

Gaudi, the great Spanish architect, moulded his cathedral in Barcelona like a miraculous piece of sculpture. Inspiration was from the heart, not the head. Unlike the great architects before him, he needed no reference, academic or otherwise. Maufe, the designer of Guildford Cathedral, was not so sure. He re-used the traditional cruciform plan and Gothic revival theme.

The first architect to successfully explore the use of new materials was Perret. His church at Le Raincy creatively uses reinforced concrete. The most expressive religious works were those by Le Corbusier at Ronchamp and La Tourette. These two buildings are the meeting halls of the medieval and modern worlds. Le Corbusier's references to historical tradition are obvious, but where is that tradition in the Church of St Francis in Brazil, the Shrine in Indiana, or the church in Sleihage, Belgium? Where were these architects leading us? The Fire Station in Harlow could well be mistaken for another church. Why not? Liverpool Cathedral is, after all, something that might well have launched Apollo 2 to the moon. Perhaps, like the pagan times before us, we have a new god. Is it space itself? Is the cathedral of the future to be the Vehicular Assembly Building at Cape Canaveral?

Church of the Sacre Coeur, Paris, 1875-77

Natural History Museum, London, by Waterhouse, 1873-79

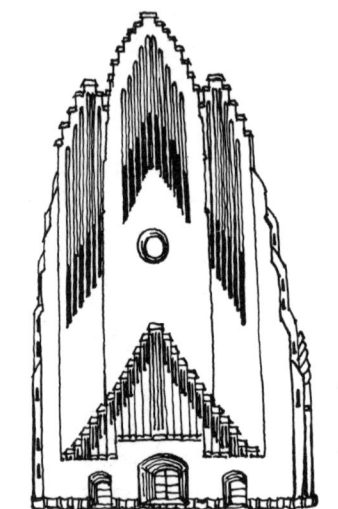

Church, Copenhagen, by Jensen Klint, 1921-26

Church of Sagrada Familia, Barcelona, by Antoni Gaudi, 1903-26. It is profusely decorated with sculptured naturalistic floral and figure ornament. Largely unfinished, it is one of the most dramatic and eccentric buildings.

Guildford Cathedral, Surrey, by Edward Maufe, 1939-61

Chapel of Notre Dame, Ronchamp, by Le Corbusier, 1950-55. A free flowing plan and form, with massive battered walls, Romanesque in feel and texture

Cistercian Monastery of La Tourette, near Lyon, by Le Corbusier, 1960. The design was influenced by the Carthusian priory of Galluzzo near Florence, the Charterhouse of Ema, and the Cistercian abbey of Le Thoronet, France.

Notre Dame, Le Raincy, France, by Perret, 1922-23.

Church at Sleihage, Belgium, 1960s

St Francis, Pampulha, Brazil, by Niemeyer, 1943

Shrine, Indiana, U.S.A., by Johnson, 1960

Fire Station, Harlow, 1961

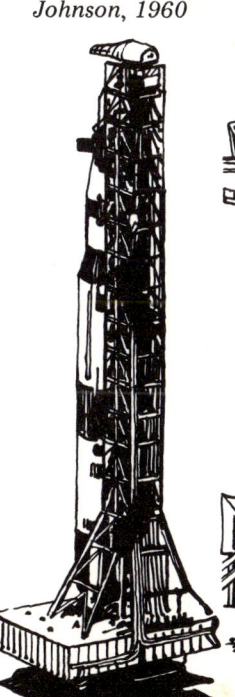

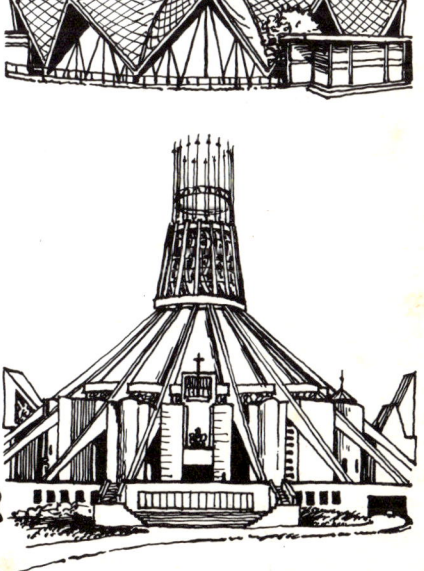

The Vehicular Assembly Building, Cape Canaveral, 1966

Apollo 2 launching pad

The Metropolitan Cathedral, Liverpool, by Sir Frederick Gibberd, 1962-67

PLACES OF WORSHIP Biographies

Leone Battista Alberti (1404-72)
Born in Italy, he was a playwright, musician, painter, mathematician, scientist and athlete as well as an architect and architectural theorist. His few buildings are all masterpieces.

Giovanni Lorenzo Bernini (1598-1680)
Italian architect and sculptor, and one of the leading figures of the Baroque movement in Rome. One of his major works is the magnificent colonnaded piazza to St Peter's.

Fillipo Brunelleschi (1377-1446)
Italian architect and sculptor, regarded as the founder of the Renaissance movement. His interest was more in Roman construction and engineering than their aesthetics. In 1407 he won a competition for the completion of the cathedral in Florence with a dome. He also designed the churches San Lorenzo (1420-5) and San Spirito (1444), and the Pitti Palace (c. 1435).

Michelangelo Buonarroti (1475-1564)
Italian sculptor, painter, poet and one of the greatest architects of all time. His influence on the later Baroque style was enormous, for he treated architecture from a sculptural and pictorial standpoint. He invented a new vocabulary of ornament, new and dynamic principles of composition, and an entirely new attitude to space. His major works include the remodelling of the group of buildings on the Capitoline Hill, Rome (1540 onwards), the Library for San Lorenzo, Florence (1524), and the completion of St Peter's, Rome (1546-64) with his design for the magnificent dome.

Antoni Gaudi (1852-1926)
The son of a coppersmith and pot and kettle maker, he was one of the most extraordinary and flamboyant Spanish architects. The lessons learnt from his father's ornamental invention flourished in his design for the church of Sagrada Familia, Barcelona. The architecture is entirely free and asymmetrical.

James Gibbs (1682-1754)
British architect and writer on architecture. Travelled extensively in Italy. His masterpiece is the domed Radcliffe Library at Oxford. He designed numerous London churches.

Baldassare Longhena (1598-1682)
Born in Venice, he started his working life as a mason. He later became a pupil of Scamozzi. His masterpiece is the church of Santa Maria della Salute.

Le Corbusier (1887-1965)
French architect, writer, painter, sculptor, town planner. One of the greatest and most influential architects of the 20th century. He wrote several pioneering books on architecture and town planning as well as producing a remarkable range of buildings and projects.

J. H. Mansart (1646-1708)
The grand-nephew of the architect Francois Mansart, he took over the work at Versailles after Le Vau's death. He was appointed Royal Architect in 1675. His work owed much to Le Vau.

Oscar Niemeyer (1907-   )
The leading modern architect in Brazil, he is influenced by Le Corbusier, with whom he worked in 1936. He is the architect of the new city Brazilia.

Balthazar Newman (1687-1753)
Born in Bohemia, he was a brilliant exponent of the Baroque style. His work consisted mainly of mansions, monasteries and churches.

Andrea Palladio (1518-1580)
Italian architect and writer who became a major influence on the architecture in England and Europe in the 17th and 18th centuries. He made an intensive study of the buildings of ancient Rome, which he later published in an influential book, *The Four Books of Architecture* (1570).

Auguste Perret (1874-1954)
Born in Brussels, he was one of the pioneers of reinforced concrete construction.

Sir George Gilbert Scott (1811-1878)
The son of a poor village clergyman, Scott became the most prominent figure of mid-19th century English architecture. He was a restorer of cathedrals and parish churches. His international reputation was based on his winning a competition for the designs of St Nicholas in Hamburg in 1844. His own buildings were Gothic in style. Of the churches he designed the most notable were St Giles, Camberwell, London (1844), and Christ Church, Ealing, London (1852).

Sir Christopher Wren (1632-1723)
The son of a clergyman, he was a scientist as well as being the greatest English architect. After a brilliant career as a scientist and mathematician at Oxford, he became a Professor of Astronomy in 1657. He did not turn to architecture until 1662, when he designed the chapel of Pembroke College, Oxford. He built 52 London churches as well as St Paul's Cathedral following the Great Fire (1666).